Two Artists

Dona Herweck Rice

Publishing Credits

Rachelle Cracchiolo, M.S.Ed., *Publisher*
Conni Medina, M.A.Ed., *Managing Editor*
Nika Fabienke, Ed.D., *Content Director*
Véronique Bos, *Creative Director*
Shaun N. Bernadou, *Art Director*
Carol Huey-Gatewood, M.A.Ed., *Editor*
John Leach, *Assistant Editor*
Courtney Roberson, *Senior Graphic Designer*

Image Credits: p.6 Iakov Filimonov/Alamy; p.8 Life On White/Getty Images; all other images from iStock and/or Shutterstock.

Teacher Created Materials
5301 Oceanus Drive
Huntington Beach, CA 92649-1030
www.tcmpub.com

ISBN 978-1-4938-9864-0

Printed in China
Nordica.082018.CA21800936

Which of these is

your  ,  ?

outfit

ballet dancer

Which of these is

your  ,  ?

shoe

ballet dancer

Which of these is

your  ,  ?

teacher painter

Which of these is

your  bear ,  ballet dancer ?

Which of these is

your  ,  ?

paper painter

dim.
(poco ritenuto - - - - - - -)
(poco largmente - - - - - - -
poco cresc.
dim.
p dolce
(poco ritenuto - - - - - -)

High-Frequency Words

New Words

these which
your

Review Words

is of